The
TIMELESS ROSARY

THE HOLY FAMILY AND THE
FLAME OF LOVE

The Timeless Rosary

The Holy Family and the Flame of Love

Brian Joseph Horan

Leonine Publishers
Phoenix, Arizona

Copyright © 2021 Brian Joseph Horan (timelessrosary.com)

Original illustrations preceding each mystery are copyright © 2012 Angela A. Barbalace (angelabarbalace.artspan.com)

The author has made every effort to credit sources in this book. He will happily acknowledge any images deemed to need documentation. All faithful reproductions of two-dimensional public domain works of art are in the public domain. While praying, if you find an edifying image or work of art in this book which touches your heart, the author encourages you to conduct an online search for the artist and consider supporting his or her work.

All rights reserved. No part of this book may be reproduced or transmitted in any form or by any means, electronic or mechanical, including photocopying, recording, or by any information storage or retrieval system now existing or to be invented, without written permission from the respective copyright holder(s), except for the inclusion of brief quotations in a review.

The Scripture citations used in this work are taken from the New American Bible (Washington, D.C.: World Catholic Press, 1986; part of WORDsearch CROSS e-book).

Published by

Leonine Publishers LLC

Phoenix, Arizona, USA

ISBN-13: 978-1-942190-64-6

Library of Congress Control Number: 2021914742

Printed in the United States of America

10 9 8 7 6 5 4 3 2 (Revised December 2022)

Visit us online at www.leoninepublishers.com

For more information: info@leoninepublishers.com

Acknowledgements

Patricia Anne Baylog, DM—for her inestimable help, which included countless hours of editing and revisions. She inspired me to write my thoughts on the timelessness of the Rosary mysteries and to share them with our bishop. My first thanks go out to her.

Bishop David O'Connell—for taking the time to review my book, writing the foreword, and sending it out with his blessing.

Cardinal Egan—for his letter and encouragement; and Archbishop Carlo Maria Viganò, Apostolic Nuncio—for his letter of support.

Father Michael, Father John, Father Jeff, Father Jay, Father Tim, Father Felix, Father Kelty, Father Anthony, Father Jason, and all the priests, sisters, and deacons—for reviewing the book and providing me with guidance and encouragement.

All the members of Saint Mary's prayer group—for their help with editing and proofing my manuscript.

The Ave Maria Shop, also known as the Blessed Sacrament prayer group—for their help with revisions.

Angela Barbalace—for the beautiful original artwork found throughout the book, depicting the timeless nature of the mysteries.

Leonine Publishers—for agreeing to take on the manuscript, turning my ideas into professional design work, and turning it into the book now in your hands.

Earl and Paul Alger, and Christina—for the wonderful job in making CDs for all the different Rosary blends, as well as the beautiful website at www.timelessrosary.com where the audio files can be obtained.

Ethan Stanley—for the front cover design (http://stanleydesigns.com/).

Marilyn, Vicky, David, Nancy, Cathy, Connie, Gery, and Pat—who helped make *The Timeless Rosary* beads.

I would also like to thank Monsignor McGovern, Dr. Renee Miller, Steve and Carol, Greg and Mary, Deborah, Nancy, Nathaniel, Joseph, Joann and Butch, my extended family of Gresko and Horan, and the countless other brothers and sisters in our great Communion of Saints who supplied help and hospitality or blazed a trail through their own writing, leaving a priceless road map for finding the Way back home.

I am eternally grateful, and may God bless each of you who helped with this endeavor.

Contents

Foreword
3

Prayers Before the Rosary
8

The First Sacred Mysteries
21

The Second Sacred Mysteries
29

The Third Sacred Mysteries
37

The Fourth Sacred Mysteries
45

The Fifth Sacred Mysteries
53

Prayers After the Rosary
60

The Timeless Rosary

The Holy Family and The Flame of Love

The Timeless Rosary: The Holy Family and the Flame of Love prayer blends the traditional prayers of the rosary, viewed in a timeless way, while entrusting the cause of life into the hands of our Blessed Mother Mary and our spiritual father Saint Joseph, while juxtaposing their titles given in the Church's **Litany of the Blessed Virgin Mary** and the **Litany of Saint Joseph.** These are then further juxtaposed with the titles given in the Church's **Litany of the Holy Name of Jesus,** while imploring His mercy on us. The Flame of Love Prayer is included in each Hail Mary after the word sinners. This helps us better understand God's Holy Family, which we are called to be part of, as His adopted children in Christ.

This rosary can be prayed individually or with a prayer group. It can be prayed amid the silence in an adoration chapel, while making a Holy Hour before the Blessed Sacrament. It can also be prayed while visiting a nursing home, or on the frontlines of spiritual battle, such as in front of an abortion clinic. You can pray this prayer anytime to request an outpouring of grace while invoking the intercession of Jesus, Mary, and Joseph, representatives of God's Holy Family here on earth.

May God bless all, who use *The Timeless Rosary* for prayer, with many blessings.

~ Most Reverend David M. O'Connell, C.M.

Foreword

The *Catechism of the Catholic Church* reminds us that, "the Church's devotion to the Blessed Virgin is intrinsic to Christian worship.... From the most ancient times the Blessed Virgin Mary has been honored with the title of 'Mother of God,' to whose protection the faithful fly in all their dangers and needs.... Marian prayer, such as the rosary, an 'epitome of the whole gospel,' expresses this devotion to the Virgin Mary" (*CCC,* no. 971).

This beautiful paragraph from our *Catechism* came to mind as I read *The Timeless Rosary*. The organization of prayers and the citation of scriptural references richly complement this traditional devotion Catholics knew, loved, and prayed "from the most ancient times."

As with many things in the Church's long history, the origin of the rosary is sometimes disputed. Tradition attributes its beginnings to an apparition of the Blessed Virgin Mary to Saint Dominic, who lived from AD 1170–1221. Saint Dominic founded the Order of Preachers, popularly known by the name "Dominicans." At the very least, we know that this devotion was gradually developed and fostered by members of his Order. The structure of the prayer we know today, with fifteen decades—three sets of five each, named for the Joyful, Sorrowful, and Glorious mysteries of Christ's life—became normative throughout the Catholic world by the 16th century papacy of Pope Pius V. The rosary continued unchanged for the next four centuries, with occasional prayers and meditations added or subtracted by local custom. In 2002, however, Blessed Pope John Paul II presented a fourth set of mysteries, the Luminous Mysteries, for the devotion of the faithful.

Devotion to the Blessed Virgin Mary through her rosary has served to lead many believers—and even some non-believers, thanks to this powerful prayer—to the heart of her Son, Jesus Christ. Devotion to Mary, yes, the way any son or daughter is "devoted" to his or her mother. But worship and the path offered by this *timeless* prayer are focused on the Lord Jesus Christ, the One Who first called her "Mother" and through whose intercession we pray the rosary.

The Timeless Rosary enriches what already is and has always been a rich source of grace and blessing in the Church through Marian prayer and devotion. May those who use this new prayer aid find the path to Jesus Christ through the intercession of our Blessed Mother Mary.

~Most Reverend David M. O'Connell, C.M.
Bishop of Trenton, July 2011

Rosary Reflections

The Three Hearts by Robert Puschautz, robertpuschautz.weebly.com
Prints available at stphilipinstitute.square.site/shop/2

For more information on the Flame of Love devotion, see *The Flame of Love: The Spiritual Diary of Elizabeth Kindelmann*, published by Queen of Peace Media, 2020.

The Sign of the Cross

In the Name of the Father, Son, and Holy Spirit… Amen.
We contemplate Your wounded sacred scourged body, which you suffered for love of us.

The Unity Prayer

My adorable Jesus, May our feet journey together. **May** our hands gather in unity. **May** our hearts beat in unison. **May** our souls be in harmony. **May** our thoughts be as one. **May** our ears listen to the silence together. **May** our glances profoundly penetrate each other. **May** our lips pray together to gain mercy from the Eternal Father. Amen.

O Saving Victim

O saving Victim, opening wide.
The gate of heaven to all below.
Our foes press on from every side.
Thine aid supply.
Thy strength bestow.
All praise and thanks to thee ascend.
Forevermore, blest One in Three.
O grant us life that shall not end.
In our true native land with thee. Amen.

~ Thomas Aquinas, c. 1227-1274

The Sign of the Cross

In the Name of the Father, Son, and Holy Spirit. Amen.
We contemplate your wounded sacred crowned head, which you suffered for love of us.

Before the Rosary

Come, O Holy Spirit, fill the hearts of Your faithful, and enkindle in them the fire of Your love.

V. Send forth Your Spirit, O Lord, and they shall be created.

R. And You shall renew the face of the earth.

 Let us pray.

God our Father pour out the gifts of Your Holy Spirit on the world. You sent the Spirit on Your Church to begin the teaching of the gospel: now let the Spirit continue to work in the world through the hearts of all who believe. Through Christ our Lord. Amen.

V. You, O Lord, will open my lips.

R. And my tongue shall announce Your praise.

V. Incline unto my aid, O God.

R. O Lord, make haste to help me.

V. Glory be to the Father, and to the Son, and to the Holy Spirit.

R. As it was in the beginning, is now and ever shall be, world without end. Amen.

May It Be Done Unto Me

O Mary, we ponder your Rosary this day.

Open our hearts to the mysteries we pray.

And may your *fiat* well up within,

Because of Jesus your Son who died for our sin.

So dear Lady, may it be done unto me.

Because of Christ and Calvary.

May it be done unto me.

Where He has set the captives free.

May it be done unto me.

~Linda Yack, S.F.O.
Saint Mary's Church

Lovely Lady Dressed in Blue

Lovely Lady dressed in blue, teach me how to pray!

God was just your little boy, tell me what to say!

Did you lift Him up, sometimes, gently, on your knee?

Did you sing to Him the way Mother does to me?

Did you hold His hand at night?

Did you ever try…

Telling stories of the world?

O! And did He cry?

Do you really think He cares if I tell Him things…

Little things that happen?

And do the angels' wings make a noise?

And can He hear me if I speak low?

Does He understand me now?

Tell me—for you know.

Lovely Lady dressed in blue, teach me how to pray!

God was just your little boy,

And you know The Way.

~ *Mary Dixon Thayer*

Come, Holy Spirit

Come, Holy Spirit, Creator blest,
And in our souls take up Thy rest.
Come with Thy grace and heavenly aid
To fill the hearts which Thou hast made.

O Comforter, to Thee we cry,
O heavenly gift of God Most High,
O fount of life and fire of love,
And sweet anointing from above.

Thou in Thy sevenfold gifts are known;
The finger of God's hand we own;
The promise of the Father, Thou,
Who dost the tongue with power endow.

Kindle our senses from above,
And make our hearts overflow with love,
With patience firm and virtue high,
The weaknesses of our flesh supply.

Far from us drive the foe we dread,
And grant us Thy peace instead;
So, shall we not, with Thee for guide,
Turn from the path of life aside.

Oh, may Thy grace on us bestow,
The Father and the Son to know;
And Thee, through endless times confessed,
Of both the eternal Spirit blest.

All glory while the ages run,
Be to the Father and the Son,
Who rose from death; the same to Thee,
O Holy Spirit, eternally. Amen.

Hail Star of the Sea

Hail bright star of ocean,
God's own Mother blest,
Ever sinless Virgin,
Gate of heavenly rest.

Taking that sweet Ave
Which from Gabriel came,
Peace confirm within us,
Changing Eva's name.

Break the captives' fetters,
Light on blindness pour,
All our ills expelling,
Every bliss implore.

Show thyself a Mother;
May the Word Divine,
Born for us thy Infant,
Hear our prayers through thine.

Virgin all excelling,
Mildest of the mild,
Freed from guilt, preserve us,
Pure and undefiled.

Keep our life all spotless,
Make our way secure,
Till we find in Jesus
Joy forevermore.

Through the highest heaven,
To the Almighty Three,
Father, Son, and Spirit
One same glory be. Amen.

O Mary

O Mary,
bright dawn of the new world,
Mother of the living,
to you do we entrust the cause of life:
Look down, O Mother,
upon the vast numbers
of babies not allowed to be born,
of the poor whose lives are made difficult,
of men and women
who are victims of brutal violence,
of the elderly and the sick killed
by indifference or out of misguided mercy.
Grant that all who believe in your Son
may proclaim the Gospel of life
with honesty and love to the people of our time.
Obtain for them the grace
to accept that Gospel
as a gift ever new,
the joy of celebrating it with gratitude
throughout their lives
and the courage to bear witness to it
resolutely, in order to build,
together with all people of good will,
the civilization of truth and love,
to the praise and glory of God
the Creator and lover of life.

~Saint John Paul II

Angel of God Prayer

Angel of God, my guardian dear.
To you God's love commits me here.
Ever this day be at my side.
To light and guard, to rule and guide.
Amen.

The Sign of the Cross

In the Name of the Father, Son, and Holy Spirit… Amen.

Apostles' Creed

I believe in God, the Father Almighty, Creator of Heaven and earth; and in Jesus Christ, His only Son, our Lord; (*Bow*) Who was conceived by the Holy Spirit, born of the Virgin Mary, suffered under Pontius Pilate, was crucified, died and was buried. He descended into hell. On the third day He arose again from the dead. He ascended into Heaven, and is seated at the right hand of God, the Father Almighty; from there He will come to judge the living and the dead. I believe in the Holy Spirit, the Holy Catholic Church, the communion of saints, the forgiveness of sins, the resurrection of the body, and life everlasting. Amen.

Our Father

Our Father, Who art in Heaven, hallowed be Thy name, Thy kingdom come; Thy will be done on earth as it is in Heaven. Give us this day our daily bread; and forgive us our trespasses as we forgive those who trespass against us; and lead us not into temptation but deliver us from evil. Amen.

Lord Jesus, we ask You for an increase in the gift of faith. You proclaim to us, **I Am** *the Way of Faith to the Father, through the Holy Spirit, Mary, and Joseph.*

Hail Mary, full of grace! The Lord is with Thee; blessed art thou among women, and blessed is the fruit of thy womb, Jesus. "Treasure of the Faithful," have mercy on us.

Holy Mary, Mother of God, and Saint Joseph, Head of the Holy Family, pray for us sinners. Spread the effect of grace of Thy Flame of Love over all humanity, now and at the hour of our death. Amen.

[1]Faith is the realization of what is hoped for and evidence of things not seen. [2] Because of it the ancients were well attested.

³ By faith we understand that the universe was ordered by the word of God, so that what is visible came into being through the invisible. ⁶ But without faith it is impossible to please him, for anyone who approaches God must believe that he exists and that he rewards those who seek him (**Hebrews 11:1-3, 6**).

Lord Jesus, we ask You for an increase in the gift of Hope. You proclaim to us, **I Am** *the Truth of Hope with the Father, through the Holy Spirit, Mary, and Joseph.*

Hail Mary, full of grace! The Lord is with Thee; blessed art thou among women, and blessed is the fruit of thy womb, Jesus. "**Crown of all Saints,**" **have mercy on us.**

Holy Mary, Mother of God, and Saint Joseph, Head of the Holy Family, pray for us sinners. Spread the effect of grace of Thy Flame of Love over all humanity, now and at the hour of our death. Amen.

¹⁴ For those who are led by the Spirit of God are children of God. ¹⁵ For you did not receive a spirit of slavery to fall back into fear, but you received a spirit of adoption, through which we cry, "Abba, Father!" The Spirit itself bears witness with our spirit that we are children of God, ¹⁷ and if children, then heirs, heirs of God and joint heirs with Christ, if only we suffer with him so that we may also be glorified with him. ¹⁸ I consider that the sufferings of this present time are as nothing com- pared with the glory to be revealed for us. ¹⁹ For creation awaits with eager expectation the revelation of the children of God; ²⁰ for creation was made subject to futility, not of its own accord but because of the one who subjected it, in hope ²¹ that creation itself would be set free from slavery to corruption and share in the glorious freedom of the children of God. ²² We know that all creation is groaning in labor pains even until now; ²³ and not only that, but we ourselves, who have the first fruits of the Spirit, we also groan within ourselves as we wait for adoption, the redemption of our bodies. ²⁴ For in hope we were saved. Now hope that sees for itself is not hope. For who hopes for what one sees? ²⁵ But if we hope for what we do not see, we wait with endurance. 26 In the

same way, the Spirit too comes to the aid of our weakness; for we do not know how to pray as we ought, but the Spirit itself intercedes with inexpressible groaning. ²⁷ And the one who searches hearts knows what the intention of the Spirit is, because it intercedes for the holy ones according to God's will. ²⁸ We know that all things work for good for those who love God, who are called according to his purpose (***Romans 8:14-28***).

Lord Jesus, we ask you for an increase in the gift of Love. You proclaim to us, **I Am** *the Life of Love in the Father, through the Holy Spirit, Mary, and Joseph.*

Hail Mary, full of grace! The Lord is with Thee; blessed art thou among women, and blessed is the fruit of thy womb, Jesus. "Our Lover," have mercy on us.

Holy Mary, Mother of God, and Saint Joseph, Head of the Holy Family, pray for us sinners. Spread the effect of grace of Thy Flame of Love over all humanity, now and at the hour of our death. Amen.

¹ If I speak in humane and angelic tongues but do not have love, I am a resounding gong or a clashing cymbal. ² And if I have the gift of prophecy and comprehend all mysteries and all knowledge; if I have all faith so as to move mountains but do not have love, I am nothing. ³ If I give away everything I own, and if I hand my body over so that I may boast but do not have love, I gain nothing. ⁴ Love is patient, love is kind. It is not jealous, love is not pompous, it is not inflated, ⁵ it is not rude, it does not seek its own interests, it is not quick-tempered, it does not brood over injury, ⁶ it does not rejoice over wrongdoing but rejoices with the truth. ⁷ It bears all things, believes all things, hopes all things, and endures all things. ⁸ Love never fails. If there are prophecies, they will be brought to nothing; if tongues, they will cease; if knowledge, it will be brought to nothing. ⁹ For we know partially, and we prophesy partially, ¹⁰ but when the perfect comes, the partial will pass away. ¹¹ When I was a child, I use to talk as a child, think as a child, reason as a child; when I became a man, I put aside childish things. ¹² At present we see indistinctly, as in a

mirror but then face to face. At present I know partially; then I shall know fully, as I am fully known. ¹³ So faith, hope, and love remain, these three; but the greatest of these is love (**1 Corinthians 13:1-13**).

Glory Be

Glory be to the Father, and to the Son, and to the Holy Spirit. As it was in the beginning, is now and ever shall be, world without end. Amen.

Fatima Prayer

O my Jesus, forgive us our sins, save us from the fires of hell, and lead all souls to Heaven, especially those in most need of Your Mercy.

Miraculous Medal Prayer

O Mary, conceived without sin, pray for us who have recourse to thee. (*three times*)

Lord, have mercy on us.
Christ, have mercy on us.

Lord, have mercy on us. Christ, hear us.
Christ, graciously hear us.

God, the Father of heaven,
Have mercy on us.

God the Son, Redeemer of the world,
Have mercy on us.

God, the Holy Spirit,
Have mercy on us.

Holy Trinity, one God,
Have mercy on us.

Holy Mary,
Pray for us.

Saint Joseph,
Pray for us.

Rosary Reflections

We kiss the wound of Your Sacred Left Hand with sorrow deep and true. The Sign of the Cross…

The First Sacred Mysteries of the Rosary of Our Redemption

The joy of the Annunciation was illuminated by Your Baptism. You ransomed us through the sorrow and shedding of Your blood during the Agony in the Garden and revealed our redemption in Your glorious Resurrection. Lord Jesus, we ask You to send us Your Holy Spirit to enlighten us in our understanding of these mysteries of our redemption.

1st Sacred
Mysteries

Rosary of Our
Redemption

First Decade

Our Father, Who art in Heaven, hallowed by Thy name, Thy kingdom come; Thy will be done on earth as it is in Heaven. *Give us this day our daily bread; and forgive us our trespasses as we forgive those who trespass against us; and lead us not into temptation but deliver us from evil. Amen.*

1. Hail Mary, full of grace! The Lord is with thee; blessed art thou among women, and blessed is the fruit of thy womb, Jesus. "Son of the living God," have mercy on us. O Mary, "Holy Mother of God," and Saint Joseph, "Spouse of the Mother of God," to you do we entrust the cause of life. **Holy Mary, Mother of God, and Saint Joseph, Head of the Holy Family, pray for us sinners. Spread the effect of grace of Thy Flame of Love over all humanity, now and at the hour of our death. Amen.**

2. Hail Mary, full of grace! The Lord is with thee; blessed art thou among women, and blessed is the fruit of thy womb, Jesus. "Son of the Virgin Mary," have mercy on us. O Mary, "Holy Virgin of Virgins," and Saint Joseph, "Guardian of Virgins," to you do we entrust the cause of life. **Holy Mary, Mother of God, and Saint Joseph, Head of the Holy Family, pray for us sinners. Spread the effect of grace of Thy Flame of Love over all humanity, now and at the hour of our death. Amen.**

3. Hail Mary, full of grace! The Lord is with thee; blessed art thou among women, and blessed is the fruit of thy womb, Jesus. "Splendor of the Father," have mercy on us. O Mary, "Mother of Christ," and Saint Joseph, "Zealous Defender of Christ," to you do we entrust the cause of life. **Holy Mary, Mother of God, and Saint Joseph, Head of the Holy Family, pray for us sinners. Spread the effect of grace of Thy Flame of Love over all humanity, now and at the hour of our death. Amen.**

1st Sacred
Mysteries

Rosary of Our
Redemption

4. Hail Mary, full of grace! The Lord is with thee; blessed art thou among women, and blessed is the fruit of thy womb, Jesus. "Author of Life," have mercy on us. O Mary, "Mother of the Church," and Saint Joseph, "Protector of Holy Church," to you do we entrust the cause of life. **Holy Mary, Mother of God, and Saint Joseph, Head of the Holy Family, pray for us sinners. Spread the effect of grace of Thy Flame of Love over all humanity, now and at the hour of our death. Amen.**

5. Hail Mary, full of grace! The Lord is with thee; blessed art thou among women, and blessed is the fruit of thy womb, Jesus. "God of Peace," have mercy on us. O Mary, "Mother of Divine Grace," and Saint Joseph, "Minister of Salvation," to you do we entrust the cause of life. **Holy Mary, Mother of God, and Saint Joseph, Head of the Holy Family, pray for us sinners. Spread the effect of grace of Thy Flame of Love over all humanity, now and at the hour of our death. Amen.**

6. Hail Mary, full of grace! The Lord is with thee; blessed art thou among women, and blessed is the fruit of thy womb, Jesus. "Lover of Chastity," have mercy on us. O Mary, "Mother Most Chaste," and Saint Joseph, "Most Chaste," to you do we entrust the cause of life. **Holy Mary, Mother of God, and Saint Joseph, Head of the Holy Family, pray for us sinners. Spread the effect of grace of Thy Flame of Love over all humanity, now and at the hour of our death. Amen.**

7. Hail Mary, full of grace! The Lord is with thee; blessed art thou among women, and blessed is the fruit of thy womb, Jesus. "Purity of Virgins," have mercy on us. O Mary, "Mother Most Pure," and Saint Joseph, "Chaste Guardian of the Virgin," to you do we entrust the cause of life. **Holy Mary, Mother of God, and Saint Joseph, Head of the Holy Family, pray for us sinners. Spread the effect of grace of Thy Flame of Love over all humanity, now and at the hour of our death. Amen.**

8. Hail Mary, full of grace! The Lord is with thee; blessed art thou among women, and blessed is the fruit of thy womb, Jesus. "Meek and Humble of Heart," have mercy on us. O Mary, "Mother Inviolate," and Saint Joseph, "Guardian of the Redeemer," to you do we entrust the cause of life. **Holy Mary, Mother of God, and Saint Joseph, Head of the Holy Family, pray for us sinners. Spread the effect of grace of Thy Flame of Love over all humanity, now and at the hour of our death. Amen.**

9. Hail Mary, full of grace! The Lord is with thee; blessed art thou among women, and blessed is the fruit of thy womb, Jesus. "Model of Virtues," have mercy on us. O Mary, "Mother Undefiled," and Saint Joseph, "Servant of Christ," to you do we entrust the cause of life. **Holy Mary, Mother of God, and Saint Joseph, Head of the Holy Family, pray for us sinners. Spread the effect of grace of Thy Flame of Love over all humanity, now and at the hour of our death. Amen.**

10. Hail Mary, full of grace! The Lord is with thee; blessed art thou among women, and blessed is the fruit of thy womb, Jesus. "Most Amiable," have mercy on us. O Mary, "Mother Most Amiable," and Saint Joseph, "Most Loyal," to you do we entrust the cause of life. **Holy Mary, Mother of God, and Saint Joseph, Head of the Holy Family, pray for us sinners. Spread the effect of grace of Thy Flame of Love over all humanity, now and at the hour of our death. Amen.** You who dwell in the shelter of the Most high, who abide in the shadow of the Almighty, [2] Say to the LORD, "My refuge and fortress, my God in whom I trust." [3] God will rescue you from the fowler's snare, from the destroying plague, [4] Will shelter you with pinions, spread wings that you may take refuge; God's faithfulness is a protecting shield (***Psalm 91:1-4***).

Glory be to the Father, and to the Son, and to the Holy Spirit. *As it was in the beginning, is now and ever shall be, world without end. Amen.*

O my Jesus, forgive us our sins, save us from the fires of hell, and lead all souls to Heaven, especially those in most need of Your mercy.

O Mary, conceived without sin, pray for us who have recourse to thee.

Lord, we ask You for an increase in the gifts of the Holy Spirit that we may come to know You clearer, follow You nearer, and love You dearer.

We kiss the wound of Your Sacred Right Hand with sorrow deep and true. The Sign of the Cross…

The Second Sacred Mysteries of the Rosary of our Redemption

The joy of the Visitation was illuminated by Your miracle at the Wedding Feast of Cana. You ransomed us through the sorrow and shedding of Your blood during the Scourging at the Pillar and revealed our redemption in Your Glorious Ascension. Lord Jesus, we ask You to send us Your Holy Spirit to enlighten us in our understanding of these mysteries of our redemption.

2nd Sacred Mysteries

Rosary of Our Redemption

Second Decade

Our Father, Who art in Heaven, hallowed by Thy name, Thy kingdom come; Thy will be done on earth as it is in Heaven. *Give us this day our daily bread; and forgive us our trespasses as we forgive those who trespass against us; lead us not into temptation but deliver us from evil. Amen.*

1. Hail Mary, full of grace! The Lord is with thee; blessed art thou among women, and blessed is the fruit of thy womb, Jesus. "Most Admirable," have mercy on us. O Mary, **"Mother Most Admirable,"** and Saint Joseph, **"Most Just,"** to you do we entrust the cause of life. **Holy Mary, Mother of God, and Saint Joseph, Head of the Holy Family, pray for us sinners. Spread the effect of grace of Thy Flame of Love over all humanity, now and at the hour of our death. Amen.**

2. Hail Mary, full of grace! The Lord is with thee; blessed art thou among women, and blessed is the fruit of thy womb, Jesus. "Angel of Great Counsel," have mercy on us. O Mary, **"Mother of Good Counsel,"** and Saint Joseph, **"Light of Patriarchs,"** to you do we entrust the cause of life. **Holy Mary, Mother of God, and Saint Joseph, Head of the Holy Family, pray for us sinners. Spread the effect of grace of Thy Flame of Love over all humanity, now and at the hour of our death. Amen.**

3. Hail Mary, full of grace! The Lord is with thee; blessed art thou among women, and blessed is the fruit of thy womb, Jesus. "The Mighty God," have mercy on us. O Mary, **"Mother of our Creator,"** and Saint Joseph, **"Model of Workmen,"** to you do we entrust the cause of life. **Holy Mary, Mother of God, and Saint Joseph, Head of the Holy Family, pray for us sinners. Spread the effect of grace of Thy Flame of Love over all humanity, now and at the hour of our death. Amen.**

2nd Sacred
Mysteries

Rosary of Our
Redemption

4. Hail Mary, full of grace! The Lord is with thee; blessed art thou among women, and blessed is the fruit of thy womb, Jesus. **"Zealous for Souls,"** have mercy on us. O Mary, **"Mother of our Savior"** and Saint Joseph, **"Patron of the Afflicted,"** to you do we entrust the cause of life. **Holy Mary, Mother of God, and Saint Joseph, Head of the Holy Family, pray for us sinners. Spread the effect of grace of Thy Flame of Love over all humanity, now and at the hour of our death. Amen.**

5. Hail Mary, full of grace! The Lord is with thee; blessed art thou among women, and blessed is the fruit of thy womb, Jesus. **"Most Obedient,"** have mercy on us. O Mary, **"Virgin Most Prudent,"** and Saint Joseph, **"Most Prudent,"** to you do we entrust the cause of life. **Holy Mary, Mother of God, and Saint Joseph, Head of the Holy Family, pray for us sinners. Spread the effect of grace of Thy Flame of Love over all humanity, now and at the hour of our death. Amen.**

6. Hail Mary, full of grace! The Lord is with thee; blessed art thou among women, and blessed is the fruit of thy womb, Jesus. **"Splendor of the Father,"** have mercy on us. O Mary, **"Virgin Most Venerable,"** and Saint Joseph, **"Most Courageous,"** to you do we entrust the cause of life. **Holy Mary, Mother of God, and Saint Joseph, Head of the Holy Family, pray for us sinners. Spread the effect of grace of Thy Flame of Love over all humanity, now and at the hour of our death. Amen.**

7. Hail Mary, full of grace! The Lord is with thee; blessed art thou among women, and blessed is the fruit of thy womb, Jesus. **"King of the Patriarchs,"** have mercy on us. O Mary, **"Virgin Most Renowned,"** and Saint Joseph, **"Most Brave,"** to you do we entrust the cause of life. **Holy Mary, Mother of God, and Saint Joseph, Head of the Holy Family, pray for us sinners. Spread the effect of grace of Thy Flame of Love over all humanity, now and at the hour of our death. Amen.**

8. Hail Mary, full of grace! The Lord is with thee; blessed art thou among women, and blessed is the fruit of thy womb, Jesus. "Most Powerful," have mercy on us. O Mary, "Virgin Most Powerful," and Saint Joseph, "Most Courageous," to you do we entrust the cause of life. **Holy Mary, Mother of God, and Saint Joseph, Head of the Holy Family, pray for us sinners. Spread the effect of grace of Thy Flame of Love over all humanity, now and at the hour of our death. Amen.**

9. Hail Mary, full of grace! The Lord is with thee; blessed art thou among women, and blessed is the fruit of thy womb, Jesus. "Crown of all Saints," have mercy on us. O Mary, "Virgin Most Merciful," and Saint Joseph, "Comfort of the Afflicted," to you do we entrust the cause of life. **Holy Mary, Mother of God, and Saint Joseph, Head of the Holy Family, pray for us sinners. Spread the effect of grace of Thy Flame of Love over all humanity, now and at the hour of our death. Amen.**

10. Hail Mary, full of grace! The Lord is with thee; blessed art thou among women, and blessed is the fruit of thy womb, Jesus. "Treasure of the Faithful," have mercy on us. O Mary, "Virgin Most Faithful," and Saint Joseph, "Most Faithful," to you do we entrust the cause of life. **Holy Mary, Mother of God, and Saint Joseph, Head of the Holy Family, pray for us sinners. Spread the effect of grace of Thy Flame of Love over all humanity, now and at the hour of our death. Amen.** [5] You shall not fear the terror of the night nor the arrow that flies by day, [6] Nor the pestilence that roams in darkness, nor the plague that ravages at noon. [7] Though a thousand fall at your side, ten thousand at your right hand, near you it shall not come (***Psalm 91:5-7***).

Glory be to the Father, and to the Son, and to the Holy Spirit. *As it was in the beginning, is now and ever shall be, world without end. Amen.*

O my Jesus, forgive us our sins, save us from the fires of hell, and lead all souls to Heaven, especially those in most need of Your mercy.

O Mary, conceived without sin, pray for us who have recourse to thee.

Lord, we ask You for an increase in the gifts of the Holy Spirit that we may come to know You clearer, follow You nearer, and love You dearer.

We kiss the wound of Your Sacred Left Foot with sorrow deep and true. The Sign of the Cross…

The Third Sacred Mysteries of the Rosary of our Redemption

The joy of the Nativity was illuminated by Your proclamation of the Kingdom of God. You ransomed us through the sorrow and shedding of Your blood during the Crowning with Thorns and revealed our redemption in the Glorious Descent of the Holy Spirit. Lord Jesus, we ask You to send us Your Holy Spirit to enlighten us in our understanding of these mysteries of our redemption.

3rd Sacred
Mysteries

Rosary of Our
Redemption

Third Decade

Our Father, Who art in Heaven, hallowed by Thy name, Thy kingdom come; Thy will be done on earth as it is in Heaven. *Give us this day our daily bread; and forgive us our trespasses as we forgive those who trespass against us; and lead us not into temptation but deliver us from evil. Amen.*

1. Hail Mary, full of grace! The Lord is with thee; blessed art thou among women, and blessed is the fruit of thy womb, Jesus. "Son of Justice," have mercy on us. O Mary, "Mirror of Justice," and Saint Joseph, "Mirror of Patience," to you do we entrust the cause of life. **Holy Mary, Mother of God, and Saint Joseph, Head of the Holy Family, pray for us sinners. Spread the effect of grace of Thy Flame of Love over all humanity, now and at the hour of our death. Amen.**

2. Hail Mary, full of grace! The Lord is with thee; blessed art thou among women, and blessed is the fruit of thy womb, Jesus. "Eternal Wisdom," have mercy on us. O Mary, "Seat of Wisdom," and Saint Joseph, "Light of Patriarchs," to you do we entrust the cause of life. **Holy Mary, Mother of God, and Saint Joseph, Head of the Holy Family, pray for us sinners, spread the effect of grace of Thy Flame of Love over all humanity, now and at the hour of our death. Amen.**

3. Hail Mary, full of grace! The Lord is with thee; blessed art thou among women, and blessed is the fruit of thy womb, Jesus. "Our Refuge," have mercy on us. O Mary, "Cause of our Joy," and Saint Joseph, "Protector of Holy Church," to you do we entrust the cause of life. **Holy Mary, Mother of God, and Saint Joseph, Head of the Holy Family, pray for us sinners. Spread the effect of grace of Thy Flame of Love over all humanity, now and at the hour of our death. Amen.**

3rd Sacred
Mysteries

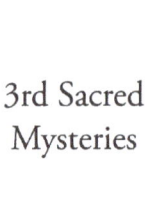

Rosary of Our
Redemption

4. Hail Mary, full of grace! The Lord is with thee; blessed art thou among women, and blessed is the fruit of thy womb, Jesus. "Treasure of the Faithful," have mercy on us. O Mary, "Spiritual Vessel," and Saint Joseph, "Patron of the Dying," to you do we entrust the cause of life. **Holy Mary, Mother of God, and Saint Joseph, Head of the Holy Family, pray for us sinners. Spread the effect of grace of Thy Flame of Love over all humanity, now and at the hour of our death. Amen.**

5. Hail Mary, full of grace! The Lord is with thee; blessed art thou among women, and blessed is the fruit of thy womb, Jesus. "Good Shepherd," have mercy on us. O Mary, "Vessel of Honor," and Saint Joseph, "Noble Offspring of David," to you do we entrust the cause of life. **Holy Mary, Mother of God, and Saint Joseph, Head of the Holy Family, pray for us sinners. Spread the effect of grace of Thy Flame of Love over all humanity, now and at the hour of our death. Amen.**

6. Hail Mary, full of grace! The Lord is with thee; blessed art thou among women, and blessed is the fruit of thy womb, Jesus. "Father of the Poor," have mercy on us. O Mary, "Singular Vessel of Devotion," and Saint Joseph, "Support in Difficulties," to you do we entrust the cause of life. **Holy Mary, Mother of God, and Saint Joseph, Head of the Holy Family, pray for us sinners. Spread the effect of grace of Thy Flame of Love over all humanity, now and at the hour of our death. Amen.**

7. Hail Mary, full of grace! The Lord is with thee; blessed art thou among women, and blessed is the fruit of thy womb, Jesus. "True Light," have mercy on us. O Mary, "Mystical Rose," and Saint Joseph, "Guardian of Virgins," to you do we entrust the cause of life. **Holy Mary, Mother of God, and Saint Joseph, Head of the Holy Family, pray for us sinners. Spread the effect of grace of Thy Flame of Love over all humanity, now and at the hour of our death. Amen.**

8. Hail Mary, full of grace! The Lord is with thee; blessed art thou among women, and blessed is the fruit of thy womb, Jesus. "Eternal Wisdom," have mercy on us. O Mary, "Tower of David," and Saint Joseph, "Noble Offspring of David," to you do we entrust the cause of life. **Holy Mary, Mother of God, and Saint Joseph, Head of the Holy Family, pray for us sinners. Spread the effect of grace of Thy Flame of Love over all humanity, now and at the hour of our death. Amen.**

9. Hail Mary, full of grace! The Lord is with thee; blessed art thou among women, and blessed is the fruit of thy womb, Jesus. "Infinite Goodness," have mercy on us. O Mary, "Tower of Ivory," and Saint Joseph, "Comfort of the Afflicted," to you do we entrust the cause of life. **Holy Mary, Mother of God, and Saint Joseph, Head of the Holy Family, pray for us sinners. Spread the effect of grace of Thy Flame of Love over all humanity, now and at the hour of our death. Amen.**

10. Hail Mary, full of grace! The Lord is with thee; blessed art thou among women, and blessed is the fruit of thy womb, Jesus. "Brightness of Eternal Light," have mercy on us. O Mary, "House of Gold," and Saint Joseph, "Light of Patriarchs," to you do we entrust the cause of life. **Holy Mary, Mother of God, and Saint Joseph, Head of the Holy Family, pray for us sinners. Spread the effect of grace of Thy Flame of Love over all humanity, now and at the hour of our death. Amen.** [8]You need simply watch the punishment of the wicked you will see. [9] You have the LORD for your refuge; you have made the Most High your stronghold. [10] No evil shall befall you, no affliction come near your tent (***Psalm 91:8-10***).

Glory be to the Father, and to the Son, and to the Holy Spirit. *As it was in the beginning, is now and ever shall be, world without end. Amen.*

O my Jesus, forgive us our sins, save us from the fires of hell, and lead all souls to Heaven, especially those in most need of Your mercy.

O Mary, conceived without sin, pray for us who have recourse to thee.

Lord, we ask You for an increase in the gifts of the Holy Spirit that we may come to know You clearer, follow You nearer, and love You dearer.

We kiss the wound of Your Sacred Right Foot with sorrow deep and true. The Sign of the Cross…

The Fourth Sacred Mysteries of the Rosary of our Redemption

The joy of the Presentation was illuminated by Your Transfiguration. You ransomed us through the sorrow and shedding of Your blood during the Carrying of the Cross and revealed our redemption in the Glorious Assumption of Your Blessed Mother into heaven. Lord Jesus, we ask You to send us Your Holy Spirit to enlighten us in our understanding of these mysteries of our redemption.

4th Sacred Mysteries

Rosary of Our Redemption

Fourth Decade

Our Father, Who art in Heaven, hallowed by Thy name, Thy kingdom come; Thy will be done on earth as it is in Heaven. *Give us this day our daily bread; and forgive us our trespasses as we forgive those who trespass against us; and lead us not into temptation but deliver us from evil. Amen.*

1. Hail Mary, full of grace! The Lord is with thee; blessed art thou among women, and blessed is the fruit of thy womb, Jesus. "Joy of the Angels," have mercy on us. O Mary, "Ark of the Covenant," and Saint Joseph, "Zealous Defender of Christ," to you do we entrust the cause of life. **Holy Mary, Mother of God, and Saint Joseph, Head of the Holy Family, pray for us sinners. Spread the effect of grace of Thy Flame of Love over all humanity, now and at the hour of our death. Amen.**

2. Hail Mary, full of grace! The Lord is with thee; blessed art thou among women, and blessed is the fruit of thy womb, Jesus. "King of Glory," have mercy on us. O Mary, "Gate of Heaven," and Saint Joseph, "Patron of the Dying," to you do we entrust the cause of life. **Holy Mary, Mother of God, and Saint Joseph, Head of the Holy Family, pray for us sinners. Spread the effect of grace of Thy Flame of Love over all humanity, now and at the hour of our death. Amen.**

3. Hail Mary, full of grace! The Lord is with thee; blessed art thou among women, and blessed is the fruit of thy womb, Jesus. "Master of the Apostles," have mercy on us. O Mary, "Morning Star," and Saint Joseph, "Model of Workmen," to you do we entrust the cause of life. **Holy Mary, Mother of God, and Saint Joseph, Head of the Holy Family, pray for us sinners. Spread the effect of grace of Thy Flame of Love over all humanity, now and at the hour of our death. Amen.**

4th Sacred Mysteries

Rosary of Our Redemption

4. Hail Mary, full of grace! The Lord is with thee; blessed art thou among women, and blessed is the fruit of thy womb, Jesus. "Most Amiable," have mercy on us. O Mary, "Health of the Sick," and Saint Joseph, "Hope of the Sick," to you do we entrust the cause of life. **Holy Mary, Mother of God, and Saint Joseph, Head of the Holy Family, pray for us sinners. Spread the effect of grace of Thy Flame of Love over all humanity, now and at the hour of our death. Amen.**

5. Hail Mary, full of grace! The Lord is with thee; blessed art thou among women, and blessed is the fruit of thy womb, Jesus. "Strength of Martyrs," have mercy on us. O Mary, "Refuge of Sinners," and Saint Joseph, "Patron of Exiles," to you do we entrust the cause of life. **Holy Mary, Mother of God, and Saint Joseph, Head of the Holy Family, pray for us sinners. Spread the effect of grace of Thy Flame of Love over all humanity, now and at the hour of our death. Amen.**

6. Hail Mary, full of grace! The Lord is with thee; blessed art thou among women, and blessed is the fruit of thy womb, Jesus. "Light of Confessors," have mercy on us. O Mary, "Comforter of the Afflicted," and Saint Joseph, "Comfort of the Afflicted," to you do we entrust the cause of life. **Holy Mary, Mother of God, and Saint Joseph, Head of the Holy Family, pray for us sinners. Spread the effect of grace of Thy Flame of Love over all humanity, now and at the hour of our death. Amen.**

7. Hail Mary, full of grace! The Lord is with thee; blessed art thou among women, and blessed is the fruit of thy womb, Jesus. "Purity of Virgins," have mercy on us. O Mary, "Help of Christians," and Saint Joseph, "Patron of the Poor," to you do we entrust the cause of life. **Holy Mary, Mother of God, and Saint Joseph, Head of the Holy Family, pray for us sinners. Spread the effect of grace of Thy Flame of Love over all humanity, now and at the hour of our death. Amen.**

8. Hail Mary, full of grace! The Lord is with thee; blessed art thou among women, and blessed is the fruit of thy womb, Jesus. "Crown of all Saints," have mercy on us. O Mary, "Queen of Angels," and Saint Joseph, "Terror of Demons," to you do we entrust the cause of life. **Holy Mary, Mother of God, and Saint Joseph, Head of the Holy Family, pray for us sinners. Spread the effect of grace of Thy Flame of Love over all humanity, now and at the hour of our death. Amen.**

9. Hail Mary, full of grace! The Lord is with thee; blessed art thou among women, and blessed is the fruit of thy womb, Jesus. "King of the Patriarchs," have mercy on us. O Mary, "Queen of Patriarchs," and Saint Joseph, "Light of Patriarchs," to you do we entrust the cause of life. **Holy Mary, Mother of God, and Saint Joseph, Head of the Holy Family, pray for us sinners. Spread the effect of grace of Thy Flame of Love over all humanity, now and at the hour of our death. Amen.**

10. Hail Mary, full of grace! The Lord is with thee; blessed art thou among women, and blessed is the fruit of thy womb, Jesus. "King of Glory," have mercy on us. O Mary, "Queen of Prophets," and Saint Joseph, "Noble Offspring of David," to you do we entrust the cause of life. **Holy Mary, Mother of God, and Saint Joseph, Head of the Holy Family, pray for us sinners. Spread the effect of grace of Thy Flame of Love over all humanity, now and at the hour of our death. Amen.** [11] For God commands the angels to guard you in all your ways. [12] With their hands they shall support you, lest you strike your foot against a stone. [13] You shall tread upon the asp and the viper; trample the lion and the dragon *(Psalm 91:12-13)*.

Glory be to the Father, and to the Son, and to the Holy Spirit. *As it was in the beginning, is now and ever shall be, world without end. Amen.*

O my Jesus, forgive us our sins, save us from the fires of hell, and lead all souls to Heaven, especially those in most need of Your mercy.

O Mary, conceived without sin, pray for us who have recourse to thee.

Lord, we ask You for an increase in the gifts of the Holy Spirit that we may come to know You clearer, follow You nearer, and love You dearer.

*We kiss the wound of Your Sacred
Side with sorrow deep and true.
The Sign of the Cross…*

The Fifth Sacred Mysteries of the Rosary of our Redemption

The joy of Finding the Child Jesus in the Temple was illuminated by Your Institution of the Eucharist. You ransomed us through the sorrow and shedding of Your blood in the Crucifixion and revealed our redemption in the Glorious Coronation of Your Blessed Mother as Queen of Heaven and Earth. Lord Jesus, we ask You to send us Your Holy Spirit to enlighten us in our understanding of these mysteries of our redemption.

5th Sacred Mysteries

Rosary of Our Redemption

FIFTH DECADE

Our Father, Who art in Heaven, hallowed by Thy name, Thy kingdom come; Thy will be done on earth as it is in Heaven. Give us this day our daily bread; and forgive us our trespasses as we forgive those who trespass against us; and lead us not into temptation but deliver us from evil. Amen.

1. Hail Mary, full of grace! The Lord is with thee; blessed art thou among women, and blessed is the fruit of thy womb, Jesus. "Brightness of Eternal Light," have mercy on us. O Mary, "Queen of the Apostles," and Saint Joseph, "Lover of Poverty," to you do we entrust the cause of life. **Holy Mary, Mother of God, and Saint Joseph, Head of the Holy Family, pray for us sinners, spread the effect of grace of Thy Flame of Love over all humanity, now and at the hour of our death. Amen.**

2. Hail Mary, full of grace! The Lord is with thee; blessed art thou among women, and blessed is the fruit of thy womb, Jesus. "King of Glory," have mercy on us. O Mary, "Queen of Martyrs," and Saint Joseph, "Most Obedient," to you do we entrust the cause of life. **Holy Mary, Mother of God, and Saint Joseph, Head of the Holy Family, pray for us sinners. Spread the effect of grace of Thy Flame of Love over all humanity, now and at the hour of our death. Amen.**

3. Hail Mary, full of grace! The Lord is with thee; blessed art thou among women, and blessed is the fruit of thy womb, Jesus. "Son of Justice," have mercy on us. O Mary, "Queen of Confessors," and Saint Joseph, "Most Prudent," to you do we entrust the cause of life. **Holy Mary, Mother of God, and Saint Joseph, Head of the Holy Family, pray for us sinners. Spread the effect of grace of Thy Flame of Love over all humanity, now and at the hour of our death. Amen.**

5th Sacred Mysteries

Rosary of Our Redemption

4. Hail Mary, full of grace! The Lord is with thee; blessed art thou among women, and blessed is the fruit of thy womb, Jesus. "Son of the Virgin Mary," have mercy on us. O Mary, "Queen of Virgins," and Saint Joseph, "Chaste Guardian of the Virgin," to you do we entrust the cause of life. **Holy Mary, Mother of God, and Saint Joseph, Head of the Holy Family, pray for us sinners. Spread the effect of grace of Thy Flame of Love over all humanity, now and at the hour of our death. Amen.**

5. Hail Mary, full of grace! The Lord is with thee; blessed art thou among women, and blessed is the fruit of thy womb, Jesus. "Crown of all Saints," have mercy on us. O Mary, "Queen of all Saints," and Saint Joseph, "Protector of Holy Church," to you do we entrust the cause of life. **Holy Mary, Mother of God, and Saint Joseph, Head of the Holy Family, pray for us sinners. Spread the effect of grace of Thy Flame of Love over all humanity, now and at the hour of our death. Amen.**

6. Hail Mary, full of grace! The Lord is with thee; blessed art thou among women, and blessed is the fruit of thy womb, Jesus. "Model of Virtues," have mercy on us. O Mary, "Queen Conceived Without Original Sin," and Saint Joseph, "Most Faithful," to you do we entrust the cause of life. **Holy Mary, Mother of God, and Saint Joseph, Head of the Holy Family, pray for us sinners. Spread the effect of grace of Thy Flame of Love over all humanity, now and at the hour of our death. Amen.**

7. Hail Mary, full of grace! The Lord is with thee; blessed art thou among women, and blessed is the fruit of thy womb, Jesus. "Zealous for Souls," have mercy on us. O Mary, "Queen Assumed into Heaven," and Saint Joseph, "Foster Father of the Son of God," to you do we entrust the cause of life. **Holy Mary, Mother of God, and Saint Joseph, Head of the Holy Family, pray for us sinners. Spread the effect of grace of Thy Flame of Love over all humanity, now and at the hour of our death. Amen.**

8. Hail Mary, full of grace! The Lord is with thee; blessed art thou among women, and blessed is the fruit of thy womb, Jesus. "The Mighty God," have mercy on us. O Mary, "Queen of the Most Holy Rosary," and Saint Joseph, "Terror of Demons," to you do we entrust the cause of life. **Holy Mary, Mother of God, and Saint Joseph, Head of the Holy Family, pray for us sinners. Spread the effect of grace of Thy Flame of Love over all humanity, now and at the hour of our death. Amen.**

9. Hail Mary, full of grace! The Lord is with thee; blessed art thou among women, and blessed is the fruit of thy womb, Jesus. "Splendor of the Father," have mercy on us. O Mary, "Queen of Families," and Saint Joseph, "Pillar of Families," to you do we entrust the cause of life. **Holy Mary, Mother of God, and Saint Joseph, Head of the Holy Family, pray for us sinners. Spread the effect of grace of Thy Flame of Love over all humanity, now and at the hour of our death. Amen.**

10. Hail Mary, full of grace! The Lord is with thee; blessed art thou among women, and blessed is the fruit of thy womb, Jesus. "Crown of all Saints," have mercy on us. O Mary, "Queen of Peace," and Saint Joseph, "Patron of the Dying," to you do we entrust the cause of life. **Holy Mary, Mother of God, and Saint Joseph, Head of the Holy Family, pray for us sinners. Spread the effect of grace of Thy Flame of Love over all humanity, now and at the hour of our death. Amen.** [14] Whoever clings to me I will deliver, whoever knows my name I will set on high. [15] All who call upon me I will answer; I will be with them in distress; I will deliver them and give them honor. [16] With length of days I will satisfy them and show them my saving power (***Psalm 91:14-16***).

Glory be to the Father, and to the Son, and to the Holy Spirit. *As it was in the beginning, is now and ever shall be, world without end. Amen.*

O my Jesus, forgive us our sins, save us from the fires of hell, and lead all souls to Heaven, especially those in most need of Your mercy.

O Mary, conceived without sin, pray for us who have recourse to thee.

Lord, we ask You for an increase in the gifts of the Holy Spirit that we may come to know You clearer, follow You nearer, and love You dearer.

Lamb of God, who takes away the sins of the world, (Spare us, O Lord Jesus.)

Lamb of God, who takes away the sins of the world, (Graciously hear us, O Lord Jesus.)

Lamb of God, who takes away the sins of the world, (Have mercy on us, O Lord Jesus.)

Psalm 105:21-22
He made him the lord of his household.
And prince over all his possessions.

Let us pray…

Grant, we beseech Thee, O Lord God, that we, your servants, may enjoy perpetual health of mind and body; and by the intercession of the Blessed Mary, ever Virgin, may be delivered from present sorrow, and obtain eternal joy. Through Christ our Lord. Amen.

Let us pray…

O God, in your ineffable providence you were pleased to choose Blessed Joseph to be the spouse of your most holy Mother. Grant, we beg you, that we may be worthy to have him for our intercessor in heaven whom on earth we venerate as our Protector: You who live and reign forever and ever, Amen.

Saint Joseph, pray for us.

Hail, Holy Queen

Hail, holy Queen, Mother of Mercy! Our life, our sweetness, and our hope! To thee do we cry, poor banished children of Eve; to thee do we send up our sighs, mourning and weeping in this valley, of tears. Turn, then, most gracious advocate, thine eyes of mercy toward us; and after this our exile show unto us the blessed fruit of thy womb, Jesus; O clement, O loving, O sweet Virgin Mary.

Pray for us, O holy Mother of God, that we may be made worthy of the promises of Christ.

Let us pray….

O God, whose only begotten Son, by His life, death, and resurrection, has purchased for us the rewards of eternal life, grant, we beseech Thee, that while meditating upon these mysteries of the Most Holy Rosary of the Blessed Virgin Mary, we may both imitate what they contain and obtain what they promise, through the same Christ our Lord. Amen.

May the divine assistance remain always with us, and may the souls of the faithful departed, through the mercy of God, rest in peace. Amen.

Saint Michael Prayer

Saint Michael, the Archangel, defend us in battle. Be our protection against the wickedness and snares of the devil. May God rebuke him, we humbly pray; and do thou, O Prince of the Heavenly Host, by the power of God, cast into hell Satan, and all the evil spirits, who prowl around the world seeking the ruin of souls. Amen.

Memorare of Saint Joseph and the Blessed Virgin Mary

Remember, O most gracious Virgin Mary and Saint Joseph, her Most Chaste Spouse, that never was it known that anyone who fled to your protection, implored your help, or sought your intercession was left unaided. Inspired by this confidence, I fly unto you, O Virgin of virgins, my mother, and Saint Joseph, my spiritual father. To you do I come. Before you do I stand, sinful and sorrowful and beg your protection. O Mother of the Word Incarnate and Saint Joseph, Foster Father of the Redeemer, despise not my petitions, but, in your mercy and goodness, hear and answer me. Amen.

Holy Virgin, with thy loving Child, thy blessings give to us this day and forever.

For the intentions of the Holy Father…

Our Father, Who art in Heaven, hallowed be Thy name, Thy kingdom come; Thy will be done on earth as it is in Heaven. Give us this day our daily bread; and forgive us our trespasses as we forgive those who trespass against us; and lead us not into temptation but deliver us from evil. Amen.
Hail Mary, full of grace! The Lord is with thee; blessed art thou among women, and blessed is the fruit of thy womb, Jesus. Holy Mary, Mother of God, and Saint Joseph, Head of the Holy Family, pray for us sinners. Spread the effect of grace of Thy Flame of Love over all humanity, now and at the hour of our death. Amen. (*three times*)

Glory be to the Father, and to the Son, and to the Holy Spirit. As it was in the beginning, is now and ever shall be, world without end. Amen.

John 1:1-18

In the beginning was the Word and the Word was with God, and the Word was God. ²He was in the beginning with God. ³All things came to be through him, and without him nothing came to be. What came to be ⁴through him was life, and this life was the light of the human race; ⁵the light shines in the darkness and the darkness has not overcome it. ⁶A man named John was sent from God. ⁷He came for testimony, to testify to the light, so that all might believe through him. ⁸He was not the light, but came to testify to the light. ⁹The true light which enlightens everyone was coming into the world. ¹⁰He was in the world, and the world came to be through him, but the world did not know him. ¹¹He came to what was his own, but his own people did not accept him. ¹² But to those who did accept Him He gave power to become children of God, to those who believe in his name, ¹³who were born not by natural generation nor by human choice nor by a man's decision but of God. ¹⁴And the Word became flesh and made his dwelling among us, and we saw his glory, the glory as of the Father's only Son, full of grace and truth. ¹⁵John testified to him and cried out, saying, "This was he of whom I said, 'The one who is coming after me ranks ahead of me because he existed before me.'" ¹⁶From his fullness we have all received, grace in place of grace, ¹⁷ Because while the law was given through Moses grace and truth came through Jesus Christ. ¹⁸No one has ever seen God. The only Son, God, who is at the Father's side, has revealed him.

Jesus, I trust in You.

                    Jesus, I trust in You.

                                      Jesus, I trust in You.

To Jesus Christ, Our Sovereign King

To Jesus Christ, our Sovereign King,
Who is the world's salvation.
All praise and homage do we bring,
And thanks and adoration.

**Christ Jesus, Victor! Christ Jesus, Ruler!
Christ Jesus, Lord and Redeemer!**

Thy reign extend, O King benign,
To every land and nation.
For in Thy kingdom, Lord divine,
Alone we find salvation.

**Christ Jesus, Victor! Christ Jesus, Ruler!
Christ Jesus, Lord and Redeemer!**

To Thee and to Thy Church, great King,
We pledge our hearts' oblation.
Until before Thy throne we sing,
In endless jubilation.

**Christ Jesus, Victor! Christ Jesus, Ruler!
Christ Jesus, Lord and Redeemer!**

After the Rosary

V. Most Sacred Heart of Jesus

R. Have mercy on us.

V. Immaculate Heart of Mary

R. Pray for us.

V. St. Joseph

R. Pray for us.

V. St. John the Evangelist

R. Pray for us.

V. St. Louis Marie de Montfort

R. Pray for us.

The Catena Legionis

Antiphon.

Who is she that comes forth as the morning rising, fair as the moon, bright as the sun, terrible as an army set in battle array?

V. My soul glorifies the Lord.

R. My spirit rejoices in God, my Savior.

V. He looks on His servant in her lowliness; henceforth, all ages will call me blessed.

R. The Almighty works marvels for me. Holy His name!

V. His mercy is from age to age, on those who fear Him.

R. He puts forth His arm in strength and scatters the proud-hearted.

V. He casts the mighty from their thrones and raises the lowly.

R. He fills the starving with good things, sends the rich away empty.

V. He protects Israel His servant, remembering His mercy,

R. The mercy promised to our fathers, to Abraham and his sons forever.

V. Glory be to the Father, and to the Son and to the Holy Spirit. *R.* As it was in the beginning is now, and ever shall be, world without end. Amen.

Antiphon.

Who is she that comes forth as the morning rising, fair as the moon, bright as the sun, terrible as an army set in battle array?

V. O Mary, conceived without sin.

R. Pray for us who have recourse to thee. (*three times*)

Let us pray.

O Lord Jesus Christ, our mediator with the Father, Who has been pleased to appoint the Most Blessed Virgin, Your mother, to be our mother also, and our mediatrix with You, mercifully grant that whoever comes to You seeking Your favors may rejoice to receive all of them through her. Amen.

Concluding Prayers

The Sign of the Cross

In the Name of the Father, Son, and Holy Spirit…Amen.

(We contemplate Your death and burial while rejoicing in Your resurrection.) **Alleluia, Alleluia, Alleluia.**

We fly to your patronage, O holy Mother of God; despise not our prayers in our necessities, but ever deliver us from all dangers, O glorious and blessed Virgin.

V. Mary Immaculate, Mediatrix of all Graces,

R. Pray for us.

V. Saints Michael, Gabriel, and Raphael,

R. Pray for us.

V. All you heavenly Powers, Mary's Legion of Angels,

R. Pray for us.

V. St. John the Baptist,

R. Pray for us.

V. Saints Peter and Paul,

R. Pray for us.

Confer, O Lord, on us, who serve beneath the standard of Mary, that fullness of faith in You and trust in her, to which it is given to conquer the world. Grant us a lively faith, animated by charity, which will lead us to perform all our actions from the motive of pure love of You, and ever to see You and serve You in our neighbor; a faith, firm and immovable as a rock, through which we shall rest tranquil and steadfast amid the crosses, toils and disappointments of life; a courageous faith which will inspire us to undertake and carry out without hesitation great things for your glory and for the salvation of souls; a faith which will be our Legion's Pillar of Fire – to lead us forth united – to kindle everywhere the fires of divine love – to enlighten those who are in darkness and in the shadow of death – to inflame those who are lukewarm – to bring back life to those who are dead in sin; and which will guide our own feet in the way of peace; so that – the battle of life over – our Legion may reassemble, without the loss of any one, in the kingdom of Your love and glory. Amen. May the souls of our departed legionaries and the souls of all the faithful departed, through the mercy of God, rest in peace. Amen.

Act of Consecration

I, N_____, a faithless sinner, renew and ratify today in thy hands the vows of my Baptism; I renounce forever Satan, his pomp's and works; and I give myself entirely to Jesus Christ, the Incarnate Wisdom, to carry my cross after Him all the days of my life, and to be more faithful to Him than I have ever been before. In the presence of all the heavenly court I choose you both this day for my Mother and Mistress, and my Spiritual Father. I deliver and consecrate to you, as thy slave, my body and soul, my goods, both interior and exterior, and even the value of all my good actions, past, present and future; leaving to you the entire and full right of disposing of me, and all that belongs to me, without exception, according to thy good pleasure, for the greater glory of God in time and in eternity.

Act of Consecration to Saint Joseph

O dearest Saint Joseph, I consecrate myself to your honor and give myself to you, that you may always be my father, my protector, and my guide in the way of salvation.

Obtain for me greater purity of heart and fervent love of the interior life.

After your example, may I do all my actions for the greater glory in union with the Divine Heart of Jesus and the Immaculate Heart of Mary.

O Blessed Saint Joseph, pray for me, that I may share in the peace and joy of your holy death.

Humbly Let Us Voice Our Homage

Humbly let us voice our homage
For so great a sacrament.
Let all former rites surrender
To the Lord's New Testament.
What the senses fail to fathom,
Let us grasp through faith's consent!

Glory, honor, adoration,
Let us sing with one accord!
Praised be God, almighty Father;
Praised be Christ, His Son, our Lord;
Praised be God, the Holy Spirit
Triune Godhead be adored! Amen.

You have given them bread from heaven: **containing in itself all delight.**

O Lord our God, may we always give due honor to the sacramental presence of the Lamb who was slain for us. May our faith be rewarded by the vision of His glory, who lives and reigns for ever and ever. Amen.

The Holy Family and the Flame of Faith 73

Divine Praises

Blessed be God.

Blessed be His Holy Name.

Blessed be Jesus Christ, true God and true Man.

Blessed be the Name of Jesus.

Blessed be His Most Sacred Heart.

Blessed be His Most Precious Blood.

Blessed be Jesus in the Most Holy Sacrament of the Altar.

Blessed be the Holy Spirit, the Consoler.

Blessed be the great Mother of God, Mary most Holy.

Blessed be her Holy and Immaculate Conception.

Blessed be her Glorious Assumption.

Blessed be the name of Mary, Virgin and Mother.

Blessed be Saint Joseph, her most chaste spouse.

Blessed be God in His Angels and in His Saints.

May the heart of Jesus, in the Most Blessed Sacrament, be praised, adored, and loved with grateful affection, at every moment, in all the tabernacles of the world, even to the end of time. Amen.

The Holy Family and the Flame of Faith 75

Holy God We Praise Thy Name

Holy God, we praise Thy name.

Lord of all, we bow before Thee!

All on earth Thy scepter claim.

All in Heaven above adore Thee.

Infinite Thy vast domain,

Everlasting is Thy reign.

Hark, the loud celestial hymn!

Angel choirs above are raising!

Cherubim and seraphim,

In unceasing chorus praising!

Fill the heavens with sweet accord:

Holy, holy, holy, Lord!

Rosary Reflections

Litany of the Blessed Virgin Mary

Lord, have mercy on us.
    Christ, have mercy on us.
Lord, have mercy on us. Christ, hear us.
    Christ, graciously hear us.
God the Father of heaven,
    have mercy on us.
God the Son, Redeemer of the world,
    have mercy on us.
God the Holy Spirit,
    have mercy on us.
Holy Trinity, one God,
    have mercy on us.
Holy Mary,
    pray for us.
Holy Mother of God,[1]
Holy Virgin of virgins,
Mother of Christ,
Mother of the Church,
Mother of divine grace,
Mother most pure,
Mother most chaste,
Mother inviolate,
Mother undefiled,
Mother most amiable,
Mother admirable,
Mother of good counsel,
Mother of our Creator,
Mother of our Saviour,
Mother of mercy,
Virgin most prudent,
Virgin most venerable,
Virgin most renowned,
Virgin most powerful,
Virgin most merciful,
Virgin most faithful,
Mirror of justice,

---

[1] Pray for us.

Seat of wisdom,
Cause of our joy,
Spiritual vessel,
Vessel of honor,
Singular vessel of devotion,
Mystical rose,
Tower of David,
Tower of ivory,
House of gold,
Ark of the Covenant,
Gate of heaven,
Morning star,
Health of the sick,
Refuge of sinners,
Comfort of the afflicted,
Help of Christians,
Queen of Angels,
Queen of Patriarchs,
Queen of Prophets,
Queen of Apostles,
Queen of Martyrs,
Queen of Confessors,
Queen of Virgins,
Queen of all Saints,
Queen conceived without original sin,
Queen assumed into heaven,
Queen of the most holy Rosary,
Queen of families,
Queen of peace.
Lamb of God, Who takes away the sins of the world,
   spare us, O Lord.
Lamb of God, Who takes away the sins of the world,
   graciously hear us, O Lord.
Lamb of God, Who takes away the sins of the world,
   have mercy on us.

Grant, we beseech Thee, O Lord God, that we, your servants, may enjoy perpetual health of mind and body; and by the intercession of the Blessed Mary, ever Virgin, may be delivered from present sorrow, and obtain eternal joy. Through Christ our Lord. Amen.

Memorare of St. Bernard

Remember, O most gracious Virgin Mary, that never was it known that anyone who fled to thy protection, implored thy help, or sought thine intercession was left unaided. Inspired by this confidence, I fly unto Thee, O Virgin of virgins, my mother; to Thee do I come, before Thee I stand, sinful and sorrowful. O Mother of the Word Incarnate, despise not my petitions, but in thy mercy hear and answer me. Amen.

Magnificat

"My soul proclaims the greatness of the Lord; my spirit rejoices in God my savior. For he has looked upon his handmaid's lowliness; behold, from now on will all ages call me blessed. The Mighty One has done great things for me, and holy is his name. His mercy is from age to age to those who fear him. He has shown might with his arm, dispersed the arrogant of mind and heart. He has thrown down the rulers from their thrones but lifted up the lowly. The hungry he has filled with good things; the rich he has sent away empty. He has helped Israel his servant, remembering his mercy, according to his promise to our fathers, to Abraham and to his descendants forever." Amen.

Angel's Prayer

"Most Holy Trinity, Father, Son, and Holy Spirit, I adore You profoundly. I offer You the most precious Body, Blood, Soul, and Divinity of Jesus Christ, present in all the tabernacles of the world, in reparation for the outrages, sacrileges and indifference by which He is offended. By the infinite merits of the Sacred Heart of Jesus and the Immaculate Heart of Mary, I beg the conversion of poor sinners."

Prayer After Communion

O Blessed Mother, upon our lips today Christ's precious blood was laid,
The blood which centuries ago was for our ransom paid;
And half in love and half in fear, we seek for aid from thee,
Lest what we worship, rapt in awe, should be profaned by me.

And would thou grant, O Mother dear, to guard these lips today,
Lessen our words and idleness and govern all we say.
Keep back the sharp and quick retorts which rise so easily,
Soften our speech with thy gentle art of sweetest charity.

For thou art ours today, by more than double right,
For a soul where Christ must dwell will be most precious in thy sight.
Thou can hardly think of us from thy dear Son apart,
So please give us from ourselves and sin, a refuge in thy heart. Amen.

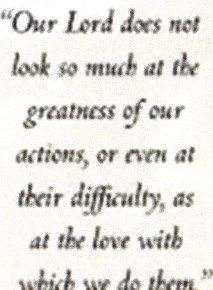

"Our Lord does not look so much at the greatness of our actions, or even at their difficulty, as at the love with which we do them."

St. Thérèse of Lisieux

Prayer for a personal consecration of individuals and groups

Eternal Father, in the Holy Spirit I want to consecrate and commit myself to the Hearts of Jesus and Mary and to be a more devoted and faithful child.

Mother Mary, today I *(name)* commit myself to your Immaculate Heart. Keep me under your maternal protection and lead me to your Son Jesus.

Lord Jesus, through the Immaculate Heart of Mary, I consecrate and commit myself to Your Sacred Heart. Mold my heart after Your heart so that You will live in me ever more. Sacred Heart of Jesus and Immaculate Heart of Mary, with this consecration and commitment I return to You the love You showed me in your earthly lives, especially on Calvary, and which you show me still today. At the same time I renew my baptismal Consecration to the triune God: I renounce sin, temptation of evil and the devil; I believe in everything that God has revealed to us and which the Catholic Church teaches us.

I promise to fulfill Jesus' commandment of love for God and my neighbor, the commandments of God and of the Church and to act according to the doctrine of the Church under the successor of St. Peter. In this way I want to contribute to the unity and growth of the Church. I will personally pray the rosary with my family and other communities and observe the devotion of the first Fridays and Saturdays, making reparation for my sins and the sins of all mankind. O Sacred Heart of Jesus and Immaculate Heart of Mary, help me to accept the Gospel in my heart and to live it in faith, hope and love, that Jesus Christ will, through His cross and resurrection, become the way, the truth and the life for me. May I be nourished on heavenly bread and live out the sacrifice of the Eucharist so that I will overcome every evil and always choose life.

Full of trust, I seek shelter in your loving hearts. Protect me in all dangers and after this earthly pilgrimage take me to my eternal home in Heaven. Amen.

Twelve Sacred Heart Promises

Every First Friday of each month, devout and faithful Catholics consecrate to the Sacred Heart of Jesus in the spirit of reparation. Jesus Christ Himself made the following promises to St. Margaret Mary Alacoque, in favor of those who fervently practice and promote this devotion.

1. I will give them all the graces necessary for their state in life.

2. I will establish peace in their families and will unite families that are divided.

3. I will comfort them in all their afflictions.

4. I will be their security and refuge during life, and especially at the hour of death.

5. I will bestow abundant blessings upon all their undertakings.

6. Sinners shall find in My Heart the source, and an infinite ocean of mercy.

7. Tepid souls shall become more fervent.

8. Fervent souls shall quickly mount to great perfection.

9. I will bless every place in which an image of My Heart shall be exposed and honored and will imprint My Love on the hearts of all those who shall wear this image on their person. I will destroy in them all disordered movements.

10. I will give the priests who are animated by a tender devotion to My Divine Heart the gift of touching the most hardened hearts.

11. Those who shall promote this devotion shall have their names written in My Heart, never to be effaced.

12. I promise you in the excess mercy of My Heart that My all powerful Love will grant to all who receive Holy Communion on the First Friday of nine consecutive months, the grace of final repentance, and that they shall not die under My displeasure, nor without receiving the Sacraments. My Heart shall be their assured refuge at that last hour.

Rosary Reflections

Our Lady's 15 Promises for Praying the Rosary

Our Lady made fifteen promises to St. Dominic and Bl. Alan de la Roche for those who pray the Rosary.

1. Whoever shall faithfully serve me by the recitation of the Rosary, shall receive signal graces.

2. I promise my special protection and the greatest graces to all those who shall recite the Rosary.

3. The Rosary shall be a powerful armor against hell, it will destroy vice, decrease sin, and defeat heresies.

4. The Rosary will cause virtue and good works to flourish; it will obtain for souls the abundant mercy of God; it will withdraw the hearts of men from the love of the world and its vanities, and will lift them to the desire for eternal things. Oh, that souls would sanctify themselves by this means.

5. The soul which recommends itself to me by the recitation of the Rosary, shall not perish.

6. Whoever shall recite the Rosary devoutly, applying himself to the consideration of its sacred mysteries shall never be conquered by misfortune. God will not chastise him in His justice, he shall not perish by an unprovided death; if he be just he shall remain in the grace of God, and become worthy of eternal life.

7. Whoever shall have a true devotion for the Rosary shall not die without the sacraments of the Church.

8. Those who are faithful to recite the Rosary shall have during their life and at their death the light of God and the plenitude of His graces; at the moment of death they shall participate in the merits of the saints in paradise.

9. I shall deliver from Purgatory those who have been devoted to the Rosary.

10. The faithful children of the Rosary shall merit a high degree of glory in Heaven.

11. You shall obtain all you ask of me by the recitation of the Rosary.

12. All those who propagate the Holy Rosary shall be aided by me in their necessities.

13. I have obtained from my Divine Son that all the advocates of the Rosary shall have for intercessors the entire celestial court during their life and at the hour of death.

14. All who recite the Rosary are my sons and daughters, and brothers and sisters of my only Son Jesus Christ.

15. Devotion of my Rosary is a great sign of predestination.

The Dove

I leave you with this final poem that was composed while in college many years ago as it sums up this soul's spiritual journey home.

I

Once upon a morning clear, while meditating far and near
Eagerly browsing through Your many pages of recorded word;
As I read with wisdom bringing air so filled with gentle singing,
And mystic sounds of winging, these were surely to be heard.
What is this? I inquired, bringing wisdom through the written word.
What is this that I've heard?

II

It was a cold and crystal February, but ah, it was extraordinary.
And not a single thought contrary in Your written word.
Patiently I communed with heaven while the angels stirred the leaven
Invoking mercy seven sevens for the sake of all who heard.
It was our long-sought message of God's eternal Word,
Here for all to be referred.

III

And Your swift and certain Light passing through my windows' sight.
Caressing me, impressing me with wisdom rarely heard.
Your message, it was so abrupt, so that now to fill my cup.
I realized I must open up to your message that I heard.
Yes to Your anointed Holy One bringing wisdom through the word.
This thought I surely must be heard.

IV

Instantly my soul grew meeker in the presence of this speaker.
Oh great and holy messenger, with such wondrous wisdom
Thou art gird.
And so gently Thou awaken, while my ignorance is shaken
And my doubts seem so mistaken, as I ponder all I've heard.
While considering with the finite, Thy infinite illuminating word
This was surely what occurred.

V

Light so very bright in seeing, into my soul, my very being,
Exploring intellect and memories in a realm quite blurred.
As Your examining proceeded, the piercing light not once retreated.
For it was not to be defeated by accusations being slurred.
Can this really be thought I, when so gently there was heard.
Fear not it is I God's own Eternal Word.

VI

Somehow I sensed You were no stranger approaching
at my humble manger.
Then again there came the whisper that I so long ago had heard.
Not so much as stalling, continuous the calling
Reminding of my falling and the love I had deterred
Yes gently whispering of the great fall that had occurred,
My separation from God's Eternal Word.

VII

As my heart lay open wide wondering what would come inside,
I was greeted by Your radiant and consoling One.
This pure and tranquil Dove gently filled my heart with Love
And Descending from above, encompassed that which was preferred.
Filling this cross of His until with His spirit was I gird,
Yes, forever was I gird.

VIII

Then Your purifying Dove inspired within me thoughts of love.
Yes, with Omnipotent and timeless Presence was He gird.
His beauty, dazzling white; with not a flaw to mar the sight,
Of Your conqueror of the night who would never be deterred.
For Thou spoke before all, "I Am Who Am," God's Eternal Word.
Yes forever, God's Eternal Word.

IX

I stood before Your Holy Spirit, hoping my mind might somehow clear it.
And reveal some distant message yet unheard.
For I could not help but see, times many facets still to be,
Changing others and changing me, and all who had incurred,
The restful Presence of this solitary Bird.
The chosen messenger of God's Eternal Word

X

For Your Dove seemed quite unique, perched on us as a cross oblique

With seven last eternal cries a remembrance of His Love is heard

These last attestations traveled high through the ages by and by.

A loving and exhausted sigh was perceived while gently heard.

Tomorrow then I shall seek this Presence much preferred.

I, too, will seek God's Eternal Word

XI

All lives storms now were calm, encompassed by Your Holy Spirit's balm.

Surely all that can be, must be in Your Word.

Passed down through the countless ages, possessing both the seers and sages,

Explaining all the written pages of history as yet unheard.

The Almighty Father returning for His lost ones, was not to be deterred.

Calling, calling, calling with His Eternal Word.

XII

But the accuser still was taking his allotted share of shaking

When into my troubled soul a thought occurred.

As one door closed for me to hide another opened from inside

While needed cleansing was applied, the gentle sound again was heard.

Who is this calmly calling courier that I've heard?

Is this really God's Eternal Word?

XIII

Then Satan's call it grew much louder, inspiring thought
of being prouder,

And not humbly acknowledging Your messenger that I'd heard.

Appealing with desire for treasure and worldly comfort
without measure,

And what of my great love of pleasure: Was this not what
I preferred?

So forget about this messenger calling through this gall-less bird.

And instead listen to my word.

XIV

He searched my memory like a tracker until my new found hope
grew blacker.

For his demons dug up every sin that had occurred.

They tried to fill me with despair and cause to doubt
God's love and care.

And what of that old affair and the punishment incurred?

Was I really ready to face the One I had perturbed?

Why not just listen to my word?

XV

Savior, said I, One of Love; Abba now in form of Dove.

Swiftly seeking the lost until the soul concurred.

No mountain He would not climb; my poor soul's Savior
so sublime.

Traveling through the sands of time, never once is He deterred.

Calling, calling, gently calling until finally He is heard,

as God's own eternal Word.

XVI

Savior, said I, One of Love; Abba now in form of Dove.

To be sought by One as great as Thee, all seems quite absurd.

Please tell this soul what it did seek on each and every mountain peak,

Why in distress it does wreak from the wandering it preferred?

To the One Who's heart was meek, The Son of God Who's gird.

As Your Eternal Word.

XVII

Be thy heart our sign of Love, Abba in the form of Dove.

Please forgive and take me home as if our parting had not occurred.

Cleanse my soul of every lie, dry the tear out from my eye.

Take me to Your endless sky and with Your Spirit gird.

To know, love, and serve Thee shall forever be preferred.

For thou art our Father, the great Eternal Word.

XVIII

Silently the Dove kept staring into my soul as if comparing,

My inner thoughts to my spoken words.

Then with a twinkling of an eye and a wondrous joyful cry,

I knew the meaning of that sigh that so long ago I'd heard.

I am a long-lost child of the Blessed Mother who incurred.

The everlasting Love of God's Eternal Word.

CREATION OF ADAM
Michelangelo, circa 1512

PIETÀ
Michelangelo, 1498-1499

Timeless Rosary Reviews

(Reviews for *The Timeless Rosary* which contains seven blends of the rosary: Praise and Worship, Spiritual Fruits, Divine Mercy, Penitential, Scriptural, Spiritual Warfare, and Meditation on the Mass.)

3339 MASSACHUSETTS AVENUE, N.W.
WASHINGTON, D.C. 20008-3610

Apostolic Nunciature
United States of America

No. 12345   October 22, 2015

Dear Brian,

        As the personal and official representative of His Holiness Pope Francis in the United States of America, I acknowledge gratefully your kind letter addressed to His Holiness Pope Francis and the accompanying two copies of your book **The Timeless Rosary**.

        Indeed, Pope Francis touched the hearts of tens of thousands of people, Catholic and non-Catholic alike, in Washington, New York, Philadelphia and beyond. As he said at the Welcoming Ceremony on the South Lawn of the White House: **"I look forward to these days of encounter and dialogue, in which I hope to listen to, and share, many of the hopes and dreams of the American people."**

        While the limitations of his official schedule prevented him from accommodating all of the wonderful requests that reached this Office, you may be sure that he felt the warmth of the good people of this vast country. At Philadelphia International Airport, just before his departure to Rome, His Holiness reflected: **"My days with you have been brief. But they have been days of great grace for me, and, I pray, for you too. Please know that as I prepare to leave, I do so with a heart full of gratitude and hope…May our days together bear fruit that will last, generosity and care for others that will endure! Just as we have received so much from God – gifts freely given us, and not of our own making – so let us freely give to others in return."**

        With renewed gratitude for your correspondence, I remain,

                                                       Sincerely yours in Christ,

                                                       Archbishop Carlo Maria Viganò
                                                       Apostolic Nuncio

RESIDENCE OF THE CARDINAL
325 EAST 33RD STREET
NEW YORK, NY 10016

October 4, 2013

Dear Brian:

Thank you most sincerely for sending me your book, *The Timeless Rosary*. It is a beautiful publication that I am sure will be a source of inspiration for many.

With gratitude and prayerful best wishes, may I remain

Very truly yours in Christ,

Edw. Card Egan

Edward Cardinal Egan
Archbishop Emeritus of New York
(*signed in his absence*)

The very essence of prayer is lifting up our hearts and minds to God, and as we pray the Rosary and meditate on its mysteries we become ever more aware of God's love for us.

Each of the Rosaries presented here, including the Praise and Worship Rosary, Spiritual Fruit Rosary, Divine Mercy Rosary, Penitential Rosary, and Timeless Scriptural Rosary, is a beautiful prayer which blends the mysteries together and can enhance our appreciation of God's Love and the events of our Redemption. I especially like the Timeless Scriptural Rosary with its accompanying Scripture passages. It would fit in very well as a part of a Holy Hour in the presence of the Blessed Sacrament. This booklet was obviously a great labor of Love, and I commend Brian for putting it together.

~Rev. Michael J. Burns
Pastor, Saint Mary's Church
Bordentown, NJ 08505

I am so very grateful to God for the blessings and powerful presence of His Holy Spirit, which fills my heart with immense joy as I not only pray, but experience the awesome wonder of His love while contemplating all the mysteries of *The Timeless Rosary*.

I have always enjoyed praying and meditating on the mysteries of the rosary. Praying and experiencing *The Timeless Rosary* only added depth to my gratitude to our beautiful God, whose light and love illuminates the path before me in the many mysteries of His love for me.

I am left in joyful awe and wonder while being humbled by the continuous power, wisdom, and guidance of His Holy Spirit who is always there for me, just a prayer away.

Praise God!

~ Deb McMullen
Devoted wife, mother of five, grandmother of one,
and humble daughter of our beautiful Lord
November 17, 2011

About five days a week I go to the fitness room in our clubhouse and usually spend one hour on the treadmill. Every treadmill has a television and is positioned in front of a window with a lovely view. At first I would watch TV for the one-hour workout. I soon realized that the time would be better spent praying the rosary. However, within a few months I found it difficult to maintain my focus and meditate on each mystery. Then Brian gave me a copy of his *Timeless Rosary*. Each treadmill has a ledge to place a book while working out. Although I fell in love with his "Penitential Rosary," I have prayed each of his "Timeless Rosaries." The blessings for me have been that I can now maintain my meditation while on the treadmill and I am only occasionally distracted with someone's greeting or loud laughter. I congratulate and thank Brian Horan for his wonderful book and I highly recommend you pray *The Timeless Rosary*.

~ Charles F. Prettyman, Prof. Emeritus
December 16, 2011

Thank you so much for sharing *The Timeless Rosary* with us. What a blessing it is. The book makes the rosary come alive and keeps you focused on the importance and details of each decade. Please let Brian know how pleased we are with this brilliant idea for renewing our dedication to saying the rosary (inspired by our Blessed Mother).

~ Patricia Koch, Parishioner

His Love Ministries is an international ministry of healing and renewal in the Roman Catholic tradition. We believe that God is Love, and this Love is Mercy; Mercy is Forgiveness; Forgiveness brings healing to our lives. The "Timeless Divine Mercy Rosary" is my favorite as it reminds us of this great truth when we pray it and meditate on God's great love for us.

~*Rev. John Campoli, I.V.Dei*
PO Box 1951
Brick, NJ 08723
908.433.4794

I had to share my thoughts and emotions with you while they are fresh. I just finished *The Timeless Rosary*.
As I prayed and got into the rhythm of the prayers, I kept my journal close. When a word in the prayer stood out to me, I wrote it in my journal for further meditation. In saying *The Timeless Rosary*, the combination and blending of the illuminations (you'll get the idea when you pray it), just stirred newness within me. I found it plugging gaps while it triggered pondering, awe and wonder.
Thanks so much for introducing this new way of praying and meditating, while growing and glowing from amazement and enlightenment. Let Brian know I will keep him in my prayers and I praise God for bringing this gift of praying to us.
Thanks again, and God Bless all of you as the Spirit gently prods you into the fullness of faith and trust in Jesus. Entering into the Rosary on my own is not the same as entering in with Mary at the doorstep, ready to walk through the mysteries beside me.
~*Pat Moore, Parishioner*

How are the four traditional Rosary prayers related to each other? Are they somehow interconnected? Which Bible verse exemplifies each mystery? Is there a way to pull everything together…to see beyond the sequential order of the mysteries…to see them truly as an interwoven, timeless prayer? From these questions, Brian Horan has found inspiration from the Holy Spirit to create *The Timeless Rosary*, giving a new depth and breadth to the Glorious, Sorrowful, Joyful, and Luminous mysteries. Although he thanks many people for helping him write this book, readers can thank him, as well, for sharing what has been his personal prayer-walk into the heart of Jesus.
~*N. Ann Ledbetter, New Jersey*

Thank you for the copy of *The Timeless Rosary* you gave to me at the Eucharistic Congress. What a beautiful presentation you have unfolded. Rarely does one experience the loving care with which every piece has been put together. The graphics, color, and binding all add up to a singular publication. I shared it with a friend who took it on her pilgrimage to the Holy Land.

As we pray the three Hail Marys before we begin the mysteries of the Rosary, we traditionally ask for the gift of Faith, Hope, and Charity (Love). I was led to modify it slightly as you will see below.

As I come to each Hail Mary, I begin with (based on John 14:6):

> I Am the Way of Faith to the Father, through the Holy Spirit, Mary and Joseph.
>
> I Am the Truth of Hope with the Father, through the Holy Spirit, Mary and Joseph.
>
> I Am the Life of Love in the Father, through the Holy Spirit, Mary and Joseph.

Surely, our Lady is pleased with the response and the author of *The Timeless Rosary*. May yet more blessings and fruit be forthcoming.

Shalom!

~ Bob Bursley

The Timeless Rosary is a wonderful new way to experience the rosary in a meaningful and expressive manner. It makes the mysteries come alive. The book brings out, to us youthful members of the Catholic faith, a powerful and pictorial view of the life of Christ and the Blessed Virgin Mary. It was easy to read and follow as it took me to a spiritual place of prayer. Thank you for giving us another way to find and strengthen our faith! With all the textbooks that I have to read in college, it is refreshing to pick up *The Timeless Rosary* and just reflect.

~ Erin M. Pease, Penn State University student

Being a person who has prayed the rosary since I was little, I was skeptical when I received a copy of *The Timeless Rosary* and a set of the CDs. But it has opened up a whole new way of getting meaning out of my prayer time. I read it when I am home or at work in my free time and when I am on the road. I put in the CD and the miles just fly by. Plus, I think that turning the drive into a prayer makes me reach my destination so much more relaxed and calm. So, yes, I am a believer that the *The Timeless Rosary* is an inspirational prayer for our time! I urge you to try it yourself."

~ Maureen T.H., College faculty member and administrator

Dear Mr. Horan,

Thank you for writing *The Timeless Rosary*. I like *The Timeless Rosary* because it is very easy to read. I'm in the 4th grade and I have to read for twenty minutes everyday except on Sunday.

When I read *The Timeless Rosary*, I get to read, pray, and write my reflections down. You might think it is going to take a long time to say and reflect on just one decade but it only really takes five minutes! I also like all the different colors. These are the reasons I like this book and think everyone should read it!

~ *Rosie McDaid, 4th grade, Saint Raphael School, Trenton, NJ*

I think *The Timeless Rosary* is a great book for believers in God or people who want to believe in God. It tells about the events when Jesus was alive.

Reading and praying this book made me feel closer to God. All the mysteries are blended together so I get the whole story each time I say a rosary. I like it that way. The reflections in between the prayers make me think about Jesus' life.

I like having the CD because if I don't have time to read the book, I can listen to the audio. Also, the CD is great for traveling. I thought the background music on the CD sounded like a beautiful choir.

I think kids will like this rosary because it will help them understand and learn about Jesus and Mary more easily as they pray.

~ *Victor Sorace, Grade 5*

About the Author

The author's mother consecrated herself to Jesus through Mary with the Saint Louis de Montfort formula before she was married. Brian Joseph Horan would, however, take much longer to follow in her footsteps by making this same consecration himself. This consecration rescued him from living in many years of sin and vice, setting him on his current path to holiness. The fourth child of five, Horan was born in Trenton, New Jersey, in October 1956. His father, James, and mother, Elizabeth, were both practicing Catholics and raised their children accordingly.

At age nineteen, Horan was involved in a near-fatal automobile accident, which left him with a severed ear, a broken jaw, and in a coma. His mother was called and told by the doctors to come to the hospital quickly, for they did not think he would survive. She hastily went to North Carolina with his sister, Maureen, spending the next three days praying the rosary by the author's side.

Horan came out of his coma on that third day, mumbling something about a beautiful Lady. He went on to recuperate fully and have a daughter of his own. He has been blessed by his daughter Maureen and son-in-law Michael, as well as two granddaughters: Remington, born a day before the Feast of Our Lady of Fatima on May 12, and Camryn, born on Our Lady's feast day, May 13.

Brian Joseph Horan became actively involved in Catholic parish life, fulfilling roles as a Reader and an Extraordinary Minister of the Eucharist. He also became an elementary school teacher for the South Hunterdon Regional School District in New Jersey, teaching primary and intermediate grades in both Stockton Borough and West Amwell elementary schools.

This book is the author's small way of thanking the Blessed Mother for the love and maternal care she showed to him and to all the children her Divine Son has redeemed.

Please visit www.timelessrosary.com for more information and to purchase audio files of *The Timeless Rosary*.

About Leonine Publishers

Leonine Publishers LLC makes fine Catholic literature available to Catholics throughout the English-speaking world. Leonine Publishers offers an innovative "hybrid" approach to book publication that helps authors as well as readers. Please visit our web site at www.leoninepublishers.com to learn more about us. Browse our online bookstore to find more solid Catholic titles to uplift, challenge, and inspire.

Our patron and namesake is Pope Leo XIII, a prudent, yet uncompromising pope during the stormy years at the close of the 19th century. Please join us as we ask his intercession for our family of readers and authors.

www.leoninepublishers.com